UNDERSTANDING PEOPLE IN SOCIETY

SOCIETY and YOU

CITIZENSHIP EDITION

Mary Cruickshank, Christina Lambert and Margaret Wilson

Series Editors:
Richard Deakin and Muir Johnstone

Published in association with

unicef

Hodder Gibson

2A Christie Street, Paisley, PA1 1NB

ACKNOWLEDGEMENTS

The authors would like to thank the following for their help in producing this book:
A. Chambers
Richard Deakin and Sam Graham
Constable Miles, Bellshill Community Police
J. O'Raw
Douglas Wilson
Jamie Cruickshank
Firefighter G. Cruickshank
Tom Wilson
UNICEF UK, in particular Heather Jarvis, Head of Education, Bruce Wilkinson, Education Officer, Scotland and Tania Sentobe, New Media and Resources.

The publishers would like to thank the following for permission to reproduce copyright photographs in this volume:
p5 340072E (Evelyn Glennie) © Rex Features Limited; p5 421076CV (Gareth Gates) © Rex Features Limited; p12 1076048 (Physiotherapist) © Photofusion; p56 10043017 (child labour) © Sean Sprague/Still Pictures; p57 003900 (Martin Luther King) © AP; BE082638 (Bob Geldof) © Corbis; p57 BE002286 (Ghandi) © Bettmann/Corbis; p57 421576AB (Nelson Mandela) © Rex Features Limited; p57 (Suffragettes) © The Illustrated New Picture Library Sph. 25 Jan 1908 cover; p58 022304 (Mother Teresa) © AP; p58 A065-1ARG (homeless) © argus/Still Pictures' p64 SP055104 (wind turbines) © Roger Tidman/Corbis; p65 1074809 (orchid) © Kjell B Sandved/Still Pictures; p75 1063812 (Phillipino girl) © Mark Edwards/Still Pictures; p76 SP1109430 (banana harvest) © Jorgen Schytte/Still Pictures; p80 Comfort Kwaasibea © Northpoint Media; p81 Mohd Usman © Rajendra Shaw; p81 La-ong © Jasda Trivittayanuruk.
Pages 41–46 and 75–76 © UNICEF UK.

Cartoons by Richard Duszczak
Illustrations by Peter Bull
Maps and diagrams by Jeff Edwards

Orders: please contact Bookpoint Ltd, 130 Milton Park, Abingdon, Oxon OX14 4SB. Telephone: (44) 01235 827720. Fax: (44) 01235 400454. Lines are open from 9.00–6.00, Monday to Saturday, with a 24-hour message answering service. You can also order through our website www.hodderheadline.co.uk.

British Library Cataloguing in Publication Data
A catalogue record for this title is available from the British Library

ISBN 0 340 814411

First Published 1998 (0340 701471)
This Edition Published 2004
Impression number   10 9 8 7 6 5 4 3 2 1
Year   2010 2009 2008 2007 2006 2005 2004
Copyright © 2004 Mary Cruickshank, Christina Lambert, Margaret Wilson

Cover photo from Corbis (CB104963)
Typeset by Fakenham Photosetting Limited, Norfolk.
Printed in Italy for Hodder Gibson, 2A Christie Street, Paisley, PA1 1NB.

CONTENTS

Preface

For the teacher

The central aim of this book and its companion text is to provide a comprehensive and adaptable programme of study for the Environmental Studies 5–14 Attainment Outcome Understanding People in Society and to promote citizenship in a global context.

The series is comprehensive in that it covers all relevant Key Features and Strands as defined in the Environmental Studies 5–14 National Guidelines published by the Scottish Executive Education Department. Since the books and their accompanying support packages provide altogether 15 self-contained study units for Understanding People in Society, there is ample scope for teachers to select and permutate units into adaptable and varied programmes of study. There are eight primary topics covering P4 to P7. The first chapter in the secondary textbook (*The World and You*) is conceived as a bridging unit incorporating P7 and S1 study programmes.

The support materials are designed to help teachers and pupils make the best use of the study package. Each chapter presented in the pupil's books has an accompanying section of support materials in the Teacher's Resource Packs: detailed syllabus plans set out clearly the People in Society Key Features and Strands covered in each unit, and offer guidance on teaching approaches and appropriate learning activities for pupils using the textbooks. Individual learning tasks are identified for specific Attainment Targets (at Levels A to F). The materials provide photocopiable helpsheets and tasksheets for use by pupils studying the units covered in the textbooks. Examples of pupil attainment records/profiles are also provided.

The Citizenship editions of Understanding People in Society are published in association with UNICEF UK (UK Registered Charity 1072612), who are eager that teachers emphasise – and pupils understand – the differentiation between needs and wants. A knowledge of our needs, rather than our wants, equips us to understand what rights are required to provide those needs, and it should be emphasised that these rights come with responsibilities that have both a local and a global dimension.

It is hoped that by using the activities contained within these books teachers can encourage children to become rights-respecting global citizens, who will work towards a fairer world with less suffering.

For pupils

You will see the following symbols throughout your textbook. Each symbol tells you something.

1 Act  Here you will have the opportunity to be an active citizen.

2 Note  You will need a pencil and paper, as you will be writing.

3 Research  You have to investigate or study something carefully.

4 Discuss  Here you will discuss ideas with a partner, with a group or as a class.

5 Question  Think carefully before you answer.

6 resource sheet You need additional factsheets/helpsheets to do this task.
SEE YOUR TEACHER.

ROSS — A CASE STUDY

Introduction

This is Ross. Ross goes to Beechwood Primary School. He is in Primary 4.

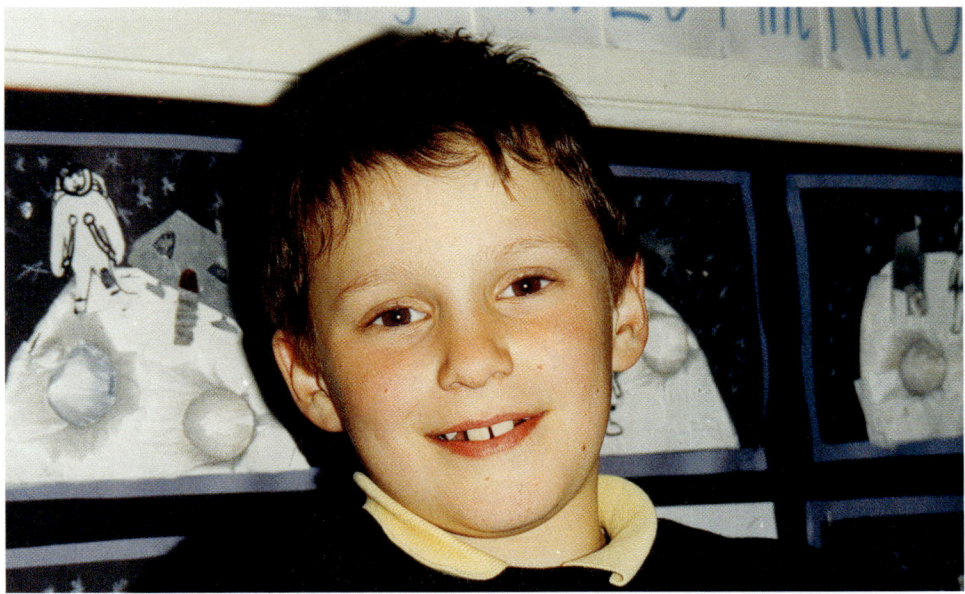

He lives with his mum and brother in a ground-floor flat.

Ross's favourite subjects at school are mathematics and PE.

His special friends are Rajab and Karen, and they often go swimming together. Karen and Ross both have computers and they are always trying to beat each other at games. Ross helps Rajab and Karen with their maths and they help push Ross to school.

Ask your teacher for Resource Sheet 1.

resource sheet

ACTIVITY

1 Make a fact sheet for yourself. Include where you live. List your likes and dislikes etc.

Ross has never been able to walk, so he needs a wheelchair to get around.

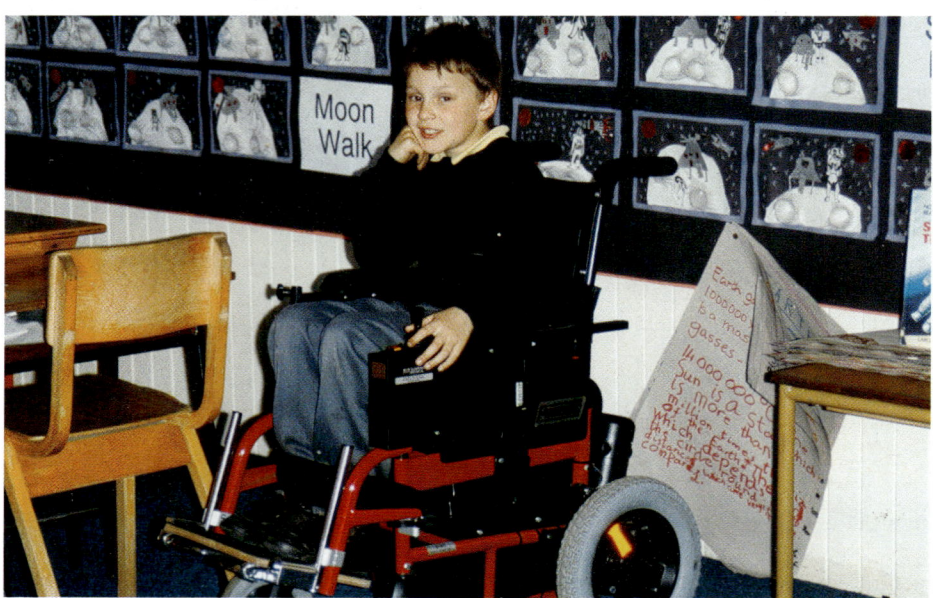

ACTIVITY

1 What things can you and Ross both do? What will Ross be able to do that you cannot do, and what will you be able to do that Ross can't?
Put your ideas into a table like this:

Ross and I can do these things	I can do these things	Ross can do these things

2 Find a partner and compare your tables before reporting back to the class.

Many people with disabilities have made great achievements and live active lives.

Although Evelyn Glennie is deaf she is a world-famous percussionist.

Even though he has a speech impediment, Gareth Gates is a successful pop idol.

Ross's home has been changed to help him. Instead of steps he has a ramp outside his home to let him go in and out easily. Who else might need changes made in their homes?

The Classroom

This is a plan of Primary 4's classroom before Ross arrived.

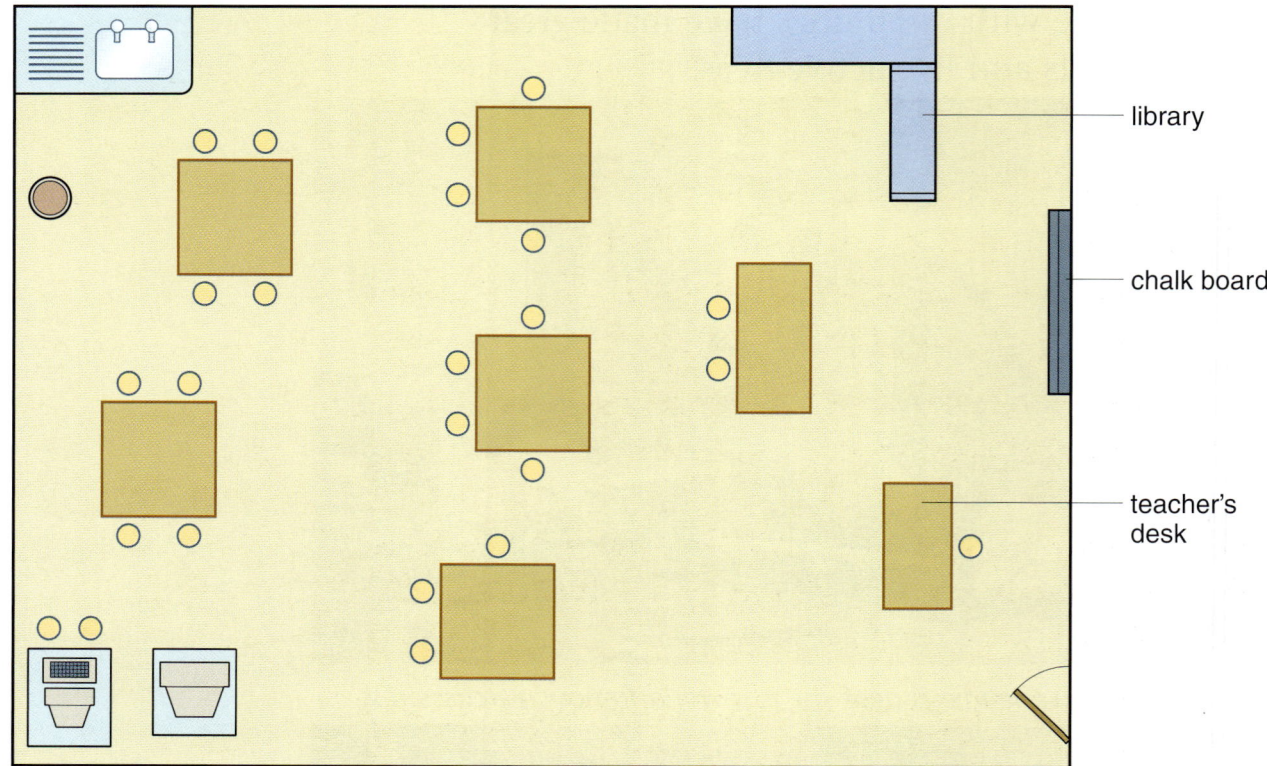

library

chalk board

teacher's desk

Some changes had to be made.

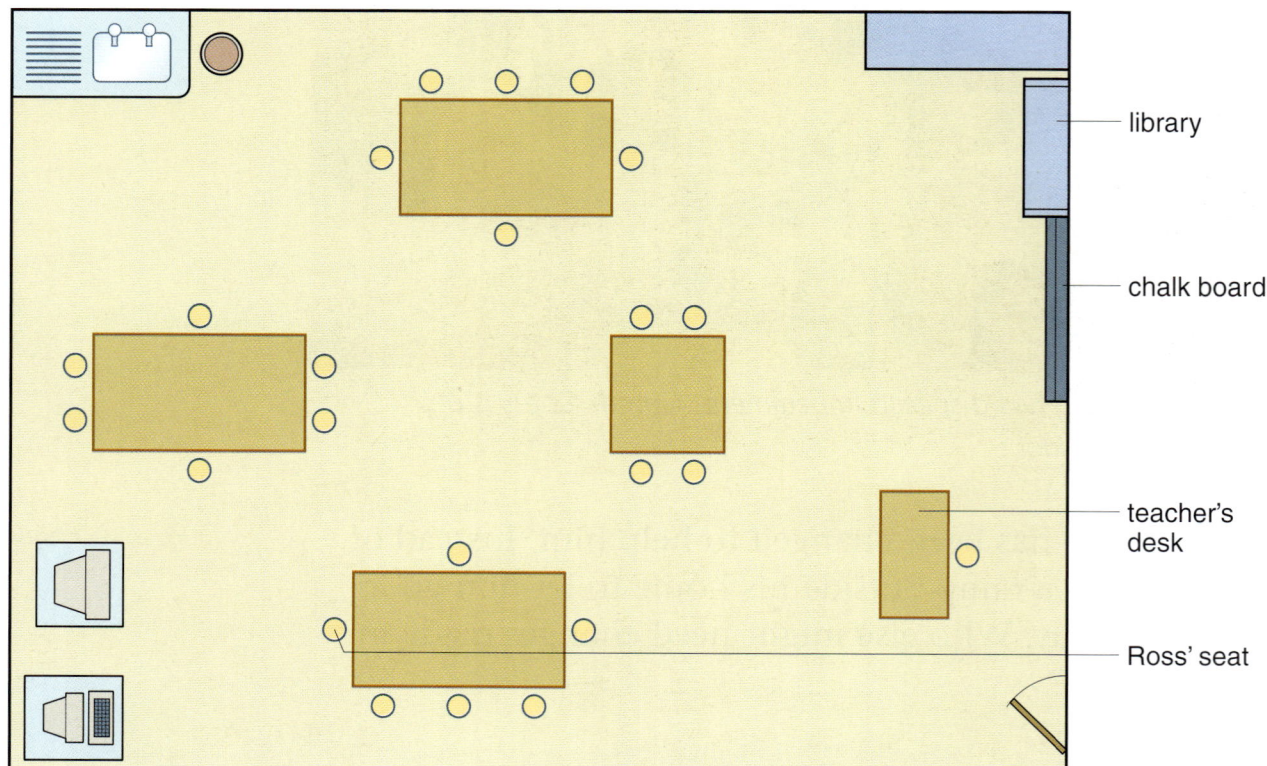

library

chalk board

teacher's desk

Ross' seat

ACTIVITY

resource *sheet*

1. What differences can you see, and why do you think these were made?

   Ask your teacher for Resource Sheet 2.

2. You will need – Resource Sheet 2 and a cut-out shape to use as the wheelchair. Plan and draw a route for Ross to return his library book and collect his jotter from the teacher's desk.

   Before you begin, label the teacher's desk, the library and Ross' seat.

When Ross is in his wheelchair the top of his head is 100 cm high. His chair is 50 cm wide. Sit on your chair and look around your class.

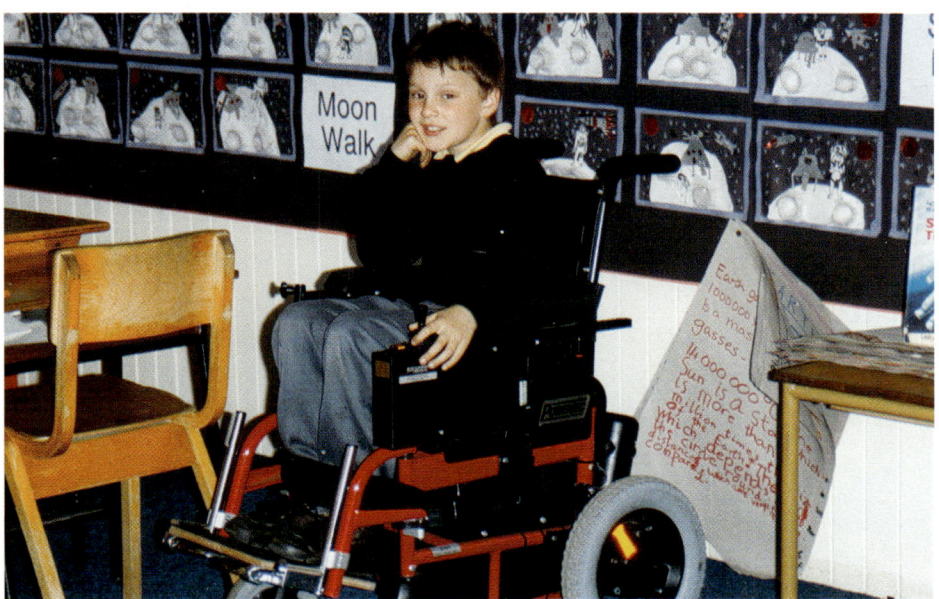

ACTIVITY

1 Can you see any problems you might have if you were in a wheelchair?

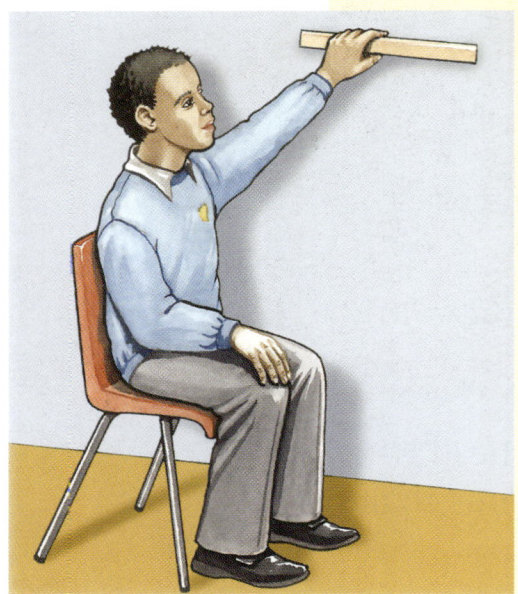

2 Measure how high you can reach when you are standing. Now sit down and measure your reach again. Choose someone and mark the level of their reach when sitting down by placing wool or strips of paper on the walls all around the room.

Make a list of things which you would no longer be able to reach if you were in a wheelchair. You can check this by sitting near these and trying to reach them.

3 Draw a plan of your classroom as it is. Mark three changes which you would make to help Ross.

4 Tell your group/class/pupil council about these changes.

The School

Beechwood Primary School

ACTIVITY

1 What differences do you notice in the entrances of these two schools? Make a list of all the differences. Why do you think they are different?

Many other changes have had to be made inside Beechwood Primary so that Ross can move around more easily and be safe just like you.

2 Take a walk around your school, looking at things you would have to change to allow Ross to move more safely from place to place. It might be helpful to make a life-size model of a wheelchair to help you with your investigation. Don't forget corridors, cloakrooms, toilets, doors and your dining room. Take notes as you go. Remember Ross can't reach or stretch as far as you.

Many people need special equipment to help them or keep them safe in school and in their homes.

3 Look for pictures and information on equipment we use to protect babies from danger; to help elderly people to get about or to do jobs about the house; to help people who have difficulty with their hearing or people who are visually impaired. Display your findings.

At Play

ACTIVITY

1 What are the children in the picture above doing? Count the number of games being played. Would Ross be able to play all of these games?

What is your favourite playtime game?

How would Ross spend his time in the playground?

2 In groups, make up a game which you could play in the playground with Ross. Remember, Ross cannot stretch as far as you or bend as low as you can. Make up rules for your own game.

Think about the equipment you will need for the game, the area you will need and how to be fair to everyone playing the game.

Spend some time considering how safe your game will be for everyone playing, including Ross.

Tell your class about your game. As a class, choose one of the games and try it out.

Fire! Fire!

One day there is a fire in Beechwood Primary and all the children have to follow their fire drill rules.

ACTIVITY

Do they:

a) let Ross go out of the class first?

b) let Ross go last?

c) let Ross go anywhere in the line?

Which do you think would be best for Ross and the class?

Make a table something like this.

	Advantages +	– Disadvantages
a. Ross first		
b. Ross last		
c. Ross in line		

Now have a vote and make a class decision.

People Who Help Us

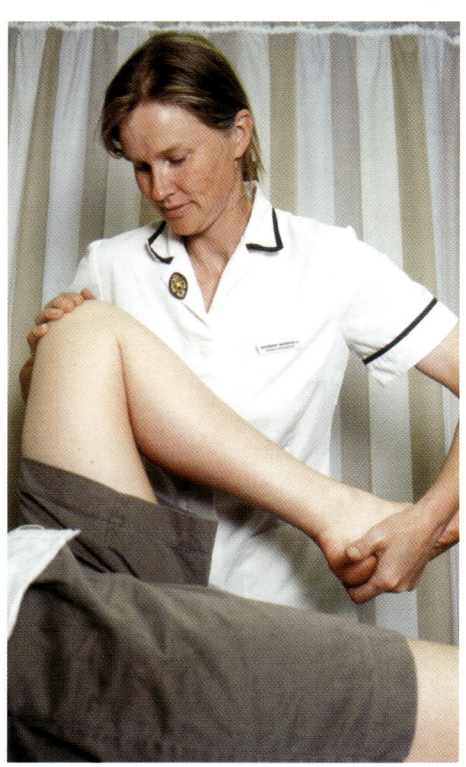

Who comes to your school to help you in different ways?

This is Mrs Ferguson. She is a **physiotherapist** and comes to school once a week to help Ross.

She helps Ross at PE with exercises to make his arms and legs stronger. Miss Scott, the class teacher, helps the rest of the class to become stronger. It is very important that Ross has exercise to stop his muscles from wasting.

ACTIVITY

1. Do you know what muscles do? If not, see if you can find out.

2. Why is exercise important for you? Which parts of your body would these forms of exercise strengthen?

Ask your teacher for Resource Sheet 3.

resource *sheet*

3. Mrs Burns also visits Ross. She is an **occupational therapist**.

   Find out what an occupational therapist does and how she might help Ross.

The Outing

Primary 4 have been doing a topic on Dinosaurs, and Miss Scott has told them that they can go on a visit to the Dino Exhibition at a museum in Edinburgh. As Ross will be going, Miss Scott has to make sure that everything will be suitable.

ACTIVITY

A. She must telephone the bus company.

1 Why? What do you think she will say?

B. She must contact the museum.

2 What will she want to know? What will she tell the museum staff?

3 Imagine the conversations Miss Scott might have had with people from the bus company and the museum. Act out one of these for the class.

4 Find out whether public buildings in your area are suitable for wheelchair users. You can do this by writing, telephoning or visiting some of these buildings.

resource
sheet

Ask your teacher for Resource Sheet 4 on which to record your findings.

Help from the Community

Primary 4 have decided to help Ross get an electric wheelchair. Other groups in the town are also fund-raising to help Ross. The class thought about what they could do to raise money. Some suggestions were made and the class voted on them, with the following results.

Idea	Votes
Bring and Buy Sale	4
Sponsored Spell	2
Car Wash	10
Sponsored Bounce	6
Sponsored Sing-a-long	4
Craft Fayre	1

Which event did the class decide on?

Now they will have to plan their event, taking care that the tasks are given out fairly and advertise it to let as many people as possible know about it.

Each child is going to design a poster which will tell people all about their event: what, when, where and why.

ACTIVITY

1 Design a poster which gives this information and will attract people to the event.

2 Can your class think of any other ways to raise money?

Fair Play

What is 'Fair Play'?

Talk about times when you have been unfair to somebody or when somebody has been unfair to you. Is there anything in your class that you think is unfair? Talk about it.

Conflict Breaker

You too can be a conflict breaker by using FAIR PLAY.

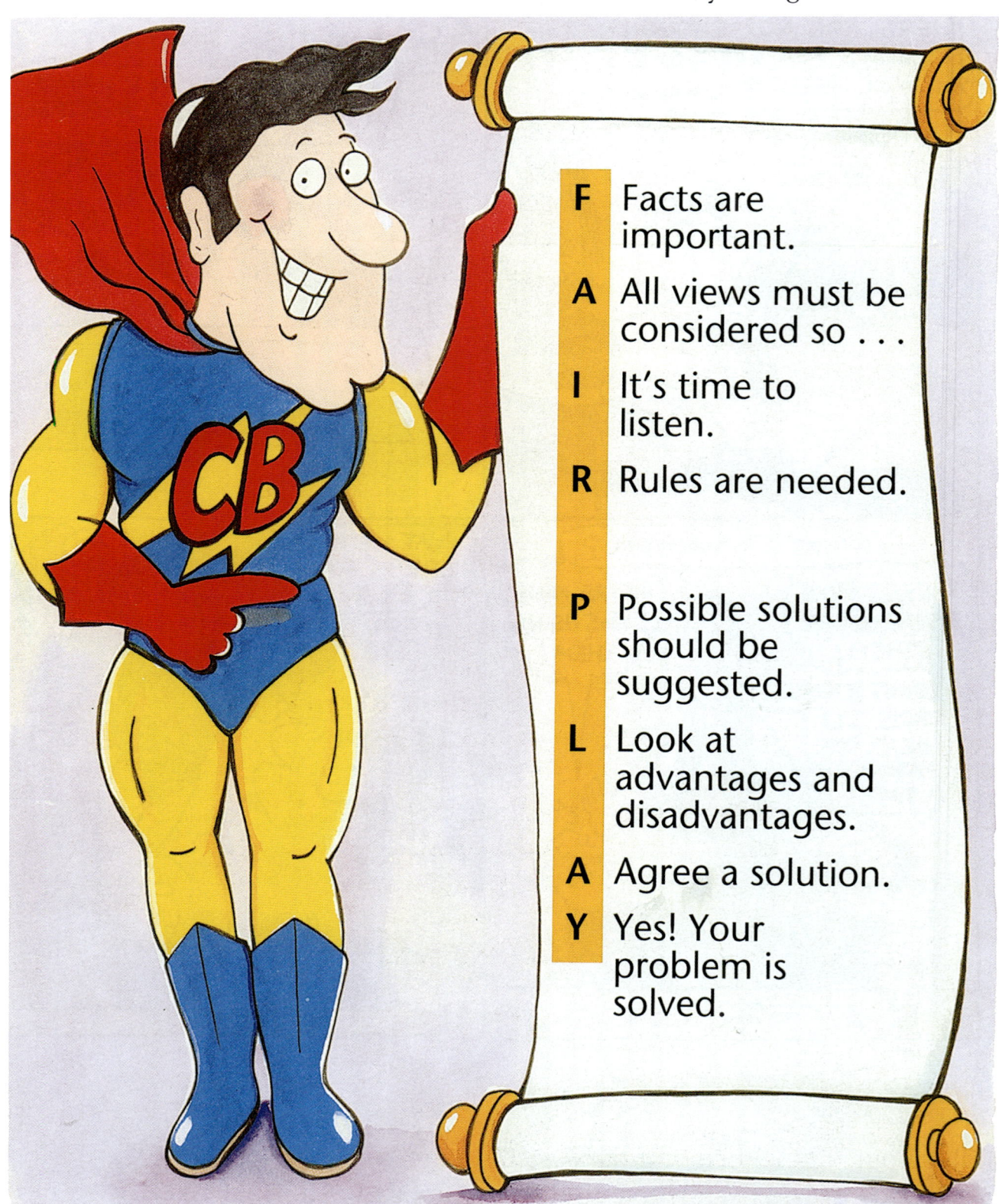

F Facts are important.

A All views must be considered so . . .

I It's time to listen.

R Rules are needed.

P Possible solutions should be suggested.

L Look at advantages and disadvantages.

A Agree a solution.

Y Yes! Your problem is solved.

Let's look at the cause of the problem between David and Fraser.

Decide

F What are the facts?
What did the teacher ask the children to do with the scissors?
Who used the scissors first?
When did Fraser lift the scissors?
What did David do?
Was he using the scissors at that moment?

A Each boy thinks he should have the scissors.

I Go into pairs, pretending you are David and Fraser.
Listen to what the other has to say, without interrupting.

R What rules could have been made in the class to avoid the situation?

P What could the boys do to solve the problem?

L Talk about the advantages and disadvantages of your ideas.

A Decide which idea would be best in this situation.

Y Yes, you have solved their problem.

Well done, PEACEMAKER.

Be a Peacemaker

ACTIVITY

1 Fiona and Morag were best friends. Every Friday, Fiona called for Morag and they walked together to Brownies. Last Friday, Fiona was slightly later than usual and when she arrived at Morag's house, Morag's mum said she had already left with Elaine, who had just moved in next door. Fiona had to walk to Brownies on her own. She felt very annoyed with Morag and started an argument. The girls haven't spoken since.

2 The Watson family were going to the school open evening, on the same evening that the Cup Final was on television. Sean wanted to see the match and decided to video it on the tape that Gran had given to him and his sister Lorna. He didn't have time to mark the tape before he left, and it was too late to watch it when he came home. After school the following day, Lorna taped her favourite soap while she went to swimming lessons. You've guessed it – she used the same tape! Sean was furious when he found out. He started shouting at her, which made Lorna angry too. By the time their mum arrived they were kicking and punching each other.

Use the FAIR PLAY code to help solve these two problems.

Stop and Think

Here are some reasons why people argue and fight:

MAKING ACCUSATIONS TEASING IDLENESS STEALING GREED THREATENING Jealousy SELFISHNESS SULKING

Can you think of any others?

Think of an argument you have had with

a) a friend   **b)** your parents.   What caused it?

What do you think causes arguments between adults?
Are the reasons the same?

Would the FAIR PLAY code help you to solve this
problem?

Here is a difficult situation between two adults.

 Ask your teacher for Resource Sheet 5. Work with a
partner.

Sometimes situations get out of hand. People end up doing things they shouldn't and in doing so can break the law and be charged with an offence. If found guilty in court, society punishes the offender in one of the following ways:

- Absolute discharge – no penalty given, no criminal offence recorded
- Admonition – no penalty given but the offence is recorded
- Compensation order – the offender has to pay compensation to the victim
- Fine – money paid to the government for a crime committed

- Probation – an offender is placed under the supervision of a probation officer to whom he or she reports on a regular basis
- Restriction of Liberty Order – an offender is electronically tagged so that they must return home by a certain time in the evening
- Community Service – an offender must give time back to society by working for no salary, for example, they may have to look after the garden of a senior citizen
- Imprisonment – an offender is locked away for a set time in a prison

MONEY, MONEY, MONEY

The Letter

One morning when Primary 5 arrived in school, they were surprised to find this letter waiting for them.

WESTERN EDUCATION AUTHORITY

Children of Primary 5,
Beechwood Primary,
Beechwood

Dear Pupils,

      Congratulations! We are delighted to announce that you are the winners of our 'Young Conservationists of the Year' award. After visiting your school, the judges were impressed by your recycling campaign. You succeeded in collecting more materials than any other entrants. We hope you will keep up this effort. We have enclosed the winning cheque for £300. We hope you enjoy planning how to spend this money.

Yours sincerely,

April Hunter

April Hunter

Conservation Projects Manager

The class were really pleased to have won, and immediately began to think of ways to spend their money.

How would your class spend £300?

Winners and Losers

The children were really happy and excited. Mr Hill, their teacher, said, 'You would think you had won a million pounds!' This set the children thinking about how people win a million pounds and whether the money makes them happy.

Think about the advantages and disadvantages of winning a million pounds.

Look at newspapers, magazines, etc. for evidence of people winning money, and how this affects the winner's life. Make a display of your evidence.

After the class had thought about millionaires, Gary pointed out that not having enough money wouldn't be much fun, and the class started to talk about this.

Think about the problems that arise from not having enough money:

a) for yourself
b) in your family
c) for your school.

Look at newspapers, magazines, etc. for evidence of poverty. Again, make a display of your evidence.

Does Money Matter?

Primary 5 decided that, while money was important, other things were equally important.

ACTIVITY

1 With a partner, make a list of all the things that you need to make you happy.

2 Organise your list under two headings:

Money Can Buy	Money Cannot Buy

Ask your teacher for Resource Sheet 6. Look at the Needs and Wants game.

3 Using Resource Sheet 6 which contains the ideas from Mr Hill's class, cut out and sort the cards under the two headings and then choose two from each list which are most important to your group.

4 Look at your 'Money can buy' list again. This time sort it into two groups: 'Needs' and 'Wants'.

What is Money?

Primary 5 were very interested in money by this time. Mr Hill agreed they should find out a bit more.

They started by looking at the collection of coins they had in their pockets. They noted similarities and differences. Almas brought some coins she used when she was in Bangladesh – and another collection was started.

Some Grandpas gave their grandchildren money which they used when they were young and which is no longer in use.

Some people brought in pesetas, francs, and lira which are no longer in use, having been replaced by the Euro.

ACTIVITY

1 Start a collection of money.

2 Sort the different types of money into sets or categories – and label.

Ask your teacher for Resource Sheet 7.

Mr Hill told the children about his granny. When she went to the cinema she paid with a jam jar – she didn't need any money.

People still swap and exchange goods and services. This is known as BARTERING.

3 Find out what people used before coins. Make notes and illustrate them. Display them in your class.

Ask your teacher for Resource Sheet 8.

Where Does Money Come From?

Primary 5 wondered how they would make money when they grew up. They had lots of different ideas. What would you like to be when you grow up? Do you think this will earn you a lot of money?

 **ACTIVITY**

Look at the following people. How do you think they got their money? Match the words to the pictures.

1 working for a boss   **5** dishonestly

2 inheritance   **6** pension

3 a lucky win   **7** self-employed

4 benefits allowances

Now read the following descriptions. Can you match these to the words and the pictures.

a) Bert goes into people's homes uninvited and helps himself to their belongings. He sells them to someone else for money.

b) Peter has recently acquired lots of money. He had a stroke of luck. He has given up his job and bought a big house.

c) Grace no longer works because she has retired. She is not as well off as she once was.

d) The Honourable Tarquin De Quincy lives in a stately

home which has belonged to his family for generations. His family's wealth means he won't have to worry about his future.

e) Colin is a nurse who works with sick children. He is paid a monthly salary.

f) Helen is a talented potter who sells her pottery from a little craft shop which she owns.

g) Patricia has two young children and is unable to work as there is no one else to look after them.

Ways of the World

Why do some people have more money than others? Is it just luck, or are there circumstances that give some people an advantage? Look at the people below and discuss the circumstances which may have helped or hindered their ability to earn money.

1.

I'm glad I'm healthy and fit and able to lift these bricks. I'm a bricklayer.

2.

I live in India. Although there were 50 children in my class, I worked very hard to pass my exams. I am a doctor.

3.

I ran away from home at 13. I got in with a bad crowd. I am a drug addict. My life is a mess.

4.

I work in a factory in Mexico. The company which employs me built their own factory in my country because they don't need to pay the people so much. They pay me less than Pedro who sits beside me, although we do the same job.

5.

My parents encouraged me to go to university, although it cost them a lot of money as they had to keep me until I was 23. I am a teacher.

6.

While I was working I paid into a retirement scheme, which now gives me extra money each month. I am a pensioner.

Put these people in order of how much money you think each has. Start with the person with the highest amount.

What is a Budget?

Having looked at the lifestyles of different people, the children of Primary 5 realised how important money is. They started to think about their own money, how they earned it, how much they got and how they spent it.

Make a chart of different ways children earn their pocket money.

Carry out a 'Pocket Money Survey' in your class and record your results on a graph.

Make a list of how you spent last week's pocket money and another of how you plan to spend next week's money.

What happens if you run out of money before the end of the week?

How do you get money to buy presents for people?

Planning ahead with money is called 'budgeting', and everyone needs to budget no matter whether they are rich or poor.

Family Budget

Families have to budget their income to make sure they meet all their needs. Although people *choose* to spend some of their money in different ways, there are certain bills which *have* to be paid by all families.

Decide which of the above items need to be paid by everyone.

Which need to be paid weekly, monthly, yearly?

Find out the different ways you can pay for items to avoid large bills.

How can families plan for special events such as birthdays, holidays or Christmas?

Taxes

Employees don't take home all the money they earn. Look at this wage slip. What deductions are made from this person's salary?

Payrun No. .... Dept No.	Week/month No. ....
Name	National Ins No. ....
Annual Salary £............ Tax code	Employee ref ....

PAYMENTS

Hours	Rate per hour	Basic pay (this month)	Deductions (this month)	Deductions (year to date)
....	£........	£.............	•Income tax £..........	£...........
			•National insurance £.........	£...........
			•Pension £........	£...........
			•Other £........	£...........

PERIOD ENDS Date :................	GROSS PAY £...............	DEDUCTIONS £...............	NET PAY £................

A wage slip

Money from deductions goes to the Government. Money from income tax is used to pay for all services provided by the Government. Money from National Insurance deductions is used to help pay for benefits – for instance retirement pensions, unemployment and sickness benefits, disability pensions. However, everyone pays taxes on many items they buy. One tax is called Value Added Tax – you will see it written as VAT.

Find out what the current rate of VAT is and what items we pay VAT on.

The Government uses the money which is collected to fund the different services which they or the local authority provide. For example:

ACTIVITY

1 With a partner or in a group, make a pictorial representation for some of the other services which the Government or local authority provides for us.

Spend, Spend, Spend!

Having learned so much about money, Primary 5 were very careful in deciding how they would spend their prize money.

The class had many ideas for how it could be spent – but not all were realistic. They decided that they needed to know how much things cost before they made a choice.

They wanted something
    for their own class,
    which everyone agreed upon and could use,
    that would last,
    and that would be fun.

They found what they wanted!

Their choice
    stayed in the class,
    was used by everyone,
    lasted for a long time
    and they had great fun!

Look at some of the catalogues which your teacher has,
and pretend you are in Primary 5 in Beechwood
Primary. How would you spend the £300?

FAMILY MATTERS

Situation 1 – The Head Teacher's Room

Emma Andrews attends Beechwood Primary but was sent home after a bullying incident. Her parents were called in to discuss the matter with the head teacher. The Andrews arrived late for their appointment and looked very harassed. The head teacher explained the situation and said that the other girl's parents were threatening to contact the police if the matter wasn't dealt with. Mr Andrews was furious with Emma.

Mr Andrews: 'This is the last straw. I've warned her . . . We have enough problems at home without this.'

Mrs Andrews: 'Leave her, Jim. You know she's having a hard time just now. We have to make allowances.'

Emma: 'I'm fed up with everything. It's always my fault!'

Head teacher: 'Let's discuss this quietly.'

Discuss: the feelings of each person in the room;
the different attitudes they have;
and
their feelings towards each other.

What do you think has been happening to make them act the way they are? Can you think of reasons why Emma is 'having a hard time' and why her mother is flustered?

resource
sheet

Everybody's behaviour affects other people. Sometimes this can be helpful and sometimes unhelpful. Use Resource Sheet 9 to

assist you in deciding which behaviours and attitudes are helpful and which are not in this situation.

Points of View

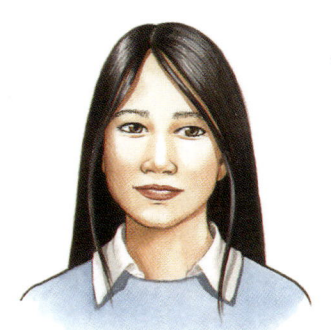

Emma: 'Gran is taking over everything. It's my bedroom but I can't play in it any more.

I don't think Gran likes me because she's always moaning at me.

I can't play my records or watch what I want to see on television.

Nobody listens to me any more.

Gran is up a lot during the night and I can't get to sleep.

I don't mean to be bossy. Nobody likes me.'

Mum: 'My mother has recently moved in with us because she isn't well enough to live on her own.

I feel a lot happier knowing that my mum is safe. If only she and Emma would try to get on a bit better.

I don't have as much time to spend on Emma and her dad, but I try to keep things going on as before.'

Dad: 'It's not fair that Emma has to share her room, but that is no excuse for her behaviour.

Emma's mum and I have tried to talk about things, but it's hard with Emma and her gran always being there.

I'm fed up with Emma moaning about her gran and Gran moaning about her. I just switch off when they start.'

The head teacher listened to Emma and her parents' different points of view. She knows how important it is to listen to all sides.

Look carefully at the statements above which Emma and her parents made to the head teacher. Make a list of facts and opinions. Put them in a table like this:

Facts	Opinions

Discuss the difficulties of sharing a room with someone. Why can sharing sometimes lead to problems?

ACTIVITY

1. What would Gran's point of view be if she were asked? Make a list of statements which you think Gran might make.

Where Do We Go from Here?

Everyone agreed that Emma had behaved badly, but that her behaviour in school was partly due to her unhappiness at home. That evening the family sat down together and discussed the situation. They made two lists. The first one contained their problems and the other listed ways of solving them. They also made a list of people whom they could contact for help.

ACTIVITY

1. Identify the main problems which the family have.

2. Find out how each of the following services can help an elderly person. How could these people help the Andrews' family?

minister of religion
doctor
social work department
Help the Aged
Age Concern etc.
local senior citizens club
health visitor
local councillor
council officials

Gran: 'When I moved in with my daughter and her family I didn't mean to be a nuisance. I didn't realise I was upsetting Emma. I certainly didn't want her to be unhappy. It was difficult to get used to not being in my own house, and I had no friends around here.

We are now on the housing list for a bigger house, and in the meantime Emma and I have come to an agreement which gives us both time on our own in the room we share. We have bought a portable television so that Emma and I can watch our favourite programmes in peace. We even have some programmes that we both like to watch and we watch those together! I go to the Day Care Centre three times a week and have started to make new friends, so I don't feel so alone now. One of the other ladies also collects me on Tuesdays and we go to the luncheon club in the local church.'

Emma: 'I know it was wrong to bully. I am sorry for what I did at school and have accepted my punishment. I am glad things are better now. Gran isn't so bad to share a room with after all.'

3 Make a list of the advantages of having a gran living with you.

Why not be an active citizen and, with your class, visit a home for senior citizens? They would love to hear you sing, recite a poem or just chat.

Situation 2 –The Head Teacher's Room

The Headteacher had an appointment with a new family whose child was coming to the school. Mr and Mrs Stewart introduced their foster daughter Ana who was to join Mr Hill's class. She was a quiet girl and the Headteacher noticed that, like all new children, she seemed very nervous about starting school.

1 Discuss ways of welcoming new children to school. If you have moved school you can tell your class about it.
- How did you feel?
- How long did it take you to settle in?
- Who or what helped you to to feel welcome?
- What did you miss about your old school?

2 Discuss how you welcome P1 pupils to your school.

Ana joined the red group in Mr Hill's class. She told everyone that she enjoyed counting and drawing, but said she found language difficult and sometimes needed help.

One afternoon in drama, Mr Hill gave the class a situation to think about. He said:

Imagine you had to leave your home due to fighting in your country. Your parents have been killed and the area in which you live is no longer safe. You decide the only thing you can do is follow the steps of others, who left some weeks before, and travel to a safe country. The nearest safe country is thousands of miles away, across the sea. You heard from your parents that others managed to get to this land by hiding in trucks. You know the journey is going to be long and dangerous but it is safer than remaining in your home country.

You had never left your country before and can't speak any other language. You feel scared and very alone. You have some money, which you use to pay an unfriendly driver in return for allowing you to hide in his dirty truck, which smells of rotting vegetables. When you get to your destination the driver kicks you out of the van and leaves you to fend for yourself.

You are on a long, deserted road – nobody is around. It starts to rain. You are very cold and hungry and you are missing your parents. You start to cry.

In groups, discuss the same questions Mr Hill gave his class to think about:

- What would you do next?
- How do you think you would feel?
- What would you miss most about your home?
- How would you go about rebuilding your life again?

Share your ideas with the rest of your class.

The child in this story was an asylum seeker.

Do you know any facts about asylum seekers and refugees? Use the true and false cards to help you find out.

Ask your teacher for the card pack on Resource Sheet 10.

You might be surprised to learn some of these facts. The ideas that you had before you played the game may not have been facts at all but opinions expressed by the media, for example, in newspapers or on television. It is important to find out the facts before making judgements.

Mr Hill surprised the class by telling them that the situation he had given them to discuss was a true story!

The brave child in the story was called Shrimana. She was from Sri Lanka and she was the girl they all knew as their new friend Ana.

The children in the class didn't know anything about Sri Lanka and wanted to find out all about Shrimana's country. Mr Hill decided they could play the "Small World" game.

Ask your teacher for the cards on Resource Sheet 11 so that you, too, can play the game.

Discuss the similarities. Try to find out other similarities between the two countries. You could display this information as a webpage or a leaflet.

Become an active citizen!

Now that you have found out some facts about asylum seekers and refugees, tell your friends and family what you have learned. Word of mouth is a very powerful way of informing other people. If everyone shared their own knowledge and corrected people when they said things that were inaccurate, we would all be much better informed.

Write a letter to someone in power or with specialist knowledge and raise an issue you feel strongly about. Ask questions you want to know the answers to. This issue may be asylum seekers or refugees or something that affects you, like litter, recycling, vandalism, bullying, drugs or wars.

Who should I write to?

This will depend on the purpose of your letter and whether you want someone to give you more information or act upon an issue. You need to find the names and addresses of key people and organisations that you want to write to. Where would you look for this information?

Some suggestions of who you could write to:

- Your local MSP
- Your local councillor
- Your local children's rights officer
- A local newspaper or young people's magazine
- Specialist organisations like UNICEF or Amnesty International or Water Aid
- Well known people you admire.

Being a member of a youth group or organisation that encourages young people to have their say helps you to become an active citizen. One way this would be possible in your school is by becoming involved in your pupil/school council.

CHILDREN'S RIGHTS

Classroom Rules

The pupils at Beechwood Primary were glad that they had rules to protect them from bullying and to keep them safe. All the classes had spent time considering their rights and responsibilities within the school to help make their school a safe and happy place.

Do you have a set of rules in your class? Are they the same as your school rules?

There may be some things in your class that you particularly like or dislike.

Make a table of things in your classroom which you like/don't like, for example:

Things I like in my classroom	Things I don't like in my classroom
1. The book corner 2. Maths	1. The curtains 2. When everyone shouts

ACTIVITY

1 As a class, collate and discuss your lists. Count the number of different things in your class that people like. Are you surprised that there are so many in this list?

But . . . let's consider the things you don't like. Some of the things cannot be changed. For example, in the list above the children cannot change the curtains, but they can stop shouting and allow each other to work quietly.

2 Now take your list of things you don't like in your classroom and rearrange it into the following table:

Things I can't change	Things I can change	Action needed
Curtains		
	People shouting	People try to talk more quietly
	Not being able to find my jotter	Keep trays tidy/label trays

ACTIVITY

1 Using your 'action needed' column to help you, decide on a set of rules for your classroom or revise your existing rules.

2 Decorate and display these rules in your classroom. Everyone in your class will be responsible for keeping these rules. Rules and responsibilities are very positive things because they protect us and give us rights.

Rule: Come into class quietly and calmly.

Responsibility:

IT IS MY RESPONSIBILITY TO WALK QUIETLY INTO CLASS !

Right:

I HAVE THE RIGHT TO FEEL SAFE IN MY SCHOOL I DON'T WANT ANYONE TO PUSH ME !

It is not only in class that children have rights. All children have rights. Rights have been around for a long time.

History of Human Rights

On the next page there is an illustration showing important dates in human rights history.

ACTIVITY

1 Match each date and graphic with the correct information below.

The Convention on the Elimination of all forms of Discrimination Against Women (CEDAW) set out the rights of women.

The Abolition of Slavery in Britain meant that no one in the British Empire could own another person.

The International Convention banning all forms of racial discrimination gives people the right to live their lives without prejudice because of their colour, race, nationality or ethnic origin.

The Universal Declaration of Human Rights is a charter drawn up by the United Nations after the horrors of the Holocaust in World War 2.

The Bill of Rights made laws more important than the wishes of the King.

The Convention relating to the Declaration of Human Rights for refugees sets out the rights of people fleeing from their own countries to seek safety elsewhere.

The UN Convention on the Rights of the Child.

The founding of the International Red Cross by Henry Dunant laid down rules to ensure the safety of ambulances, hospitals, stores and people using the Red Cross symbol.

Ask your teacher for Resource Sheet 12.

resource *sheet*

ACTIVITY

1 Your task is to make a project folder. You can choose your topic from the following: **Refugees**; **Red Cross**; **Slavery**. To make the project folder you will need some pages of paper for a small booklet. Plan the layout of your folder so that you will have a title page or cover, followed by pages of information. You can add your own illustrations, photographs or pictures to make the layout of your folder more interesting to the reader.

Look in reference books, newspapers, CDs, the Internet etc. for information and pictures. You might want to visit your local library.

2 Set a date for completion of your folder. Make a two-minute presentation to your class on your chosen topic.

resource sheet

Ask your teacher for UNICEF Resource Sheet 13.

Your rights, and the rights of all children, were set out in a UN document called a Convention. Among these, children have the right to:

travel	education	be safe from harm
health care	privacy	join clubs or groups
special care and education if they are disabled	worship as they wish	enjoy rest, leisure and play

ACTIVITY

resource sheet

1 Ask your teacher for Resource Sheet 13 and UNICEF Resource Sheets A and B (Needs and Wants cards).

2 Now you have completed this task, ask your teacher for UNICEF Resource Sheets C, D, E, F, G and H (Clustering Cards).

3 Working with a partner, choose one of the rights in the Needs and Wants game and design a logo for it. Remember, a logo is a picture representing written words. It must be clear and simple and get the meaning or message across. Try to restrict your design to two colours.

Plan your design on a small piece of paper and, when you are happy with it, enlarge it for display in your classroom.

Legal Limits

Read the following statements and then decide at what age you are legally allowed or obliged to do each of these things. Your answers can range from birth to 18 years, and you may find that the same age applies more than once.

a) withdraw money using a cash card

b) drive a car

c) receive full time education

d) change your name

e) buy fireworks

f) open a bank or business account

g) be convicted if you are aware that what you were doing was a crime

h) get married

i) get a part-time job

j) vote in an election

k) withdraw money from a National Savings Account

l) buy a pet on your own

m) buy a drink in a public bar

n) leave school

o) join a trade union

Compare your answers with a partner and then ask your teacher for the correct ages.

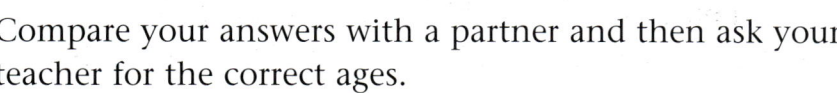

How many did you get correct? Did any of these ages surprise you? If you had the choice, would you change any of the ages? Discuss your reasons with your partner. Why do you think age limits are set for some activities? Can you think of age restrictions for any other activities?

What Rights Mean to Me

Let's look at some of your rights again. What do they mean to you personally? Jamie, a P6 pupil at Beechwood Primary, looked at his right to education, and this is what it means to him.

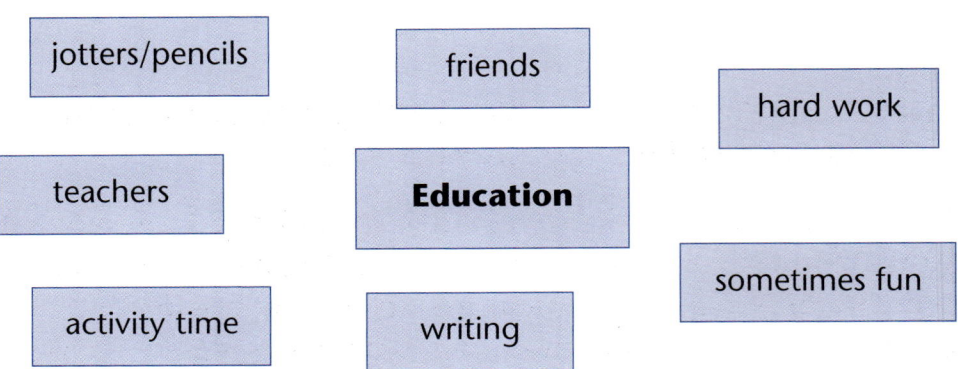

jotters/pencils

friends

hard work

teachers

Education

sometimes fun

activity time

writing

Jamie thought of different ways to display his thoughts. Here are some of them.

 Choose one of the following words: **Hobbies**; **Holidays**; **Safety**. Make a rough list of everything it means to you in your everyday life. Now choose a way to display it. You may use one of Jamie's ideas, or perhaps you can think of a better idea of your own.

Rights and Wrongs

Rights are not laws in every country, and some people do not have all the rights that we enjoy.

Long ago, children in the United Kingdom did not all go to school. Mainly rich children were educated, and in most cases only boys. Many children had to work from an early age as **chimney sweeps**, **selling things in the street**, as **factory workers** and **in coal mines**.

Choose one of the groups of children mentioned above and find out about their lives.

Hint: A good place to start your research would be in the Victorian era. ✳

In many countries in the world there are still many children working in terrible conditions who are being denied their basic human rights. Children are cheaper to employ, are more obedient and easier to train to their employer's requirements. Schooling is often considered to be too expensive and not relevant to the child's lifestyle. Many children are separated from their families and work very long hours for cruel employers.

Haiti – as many as 100,000 children from the age of five are separated from their parents to work as live-in domestic servants.

Peru – children are enslaved to extract gold in the Madre de Dios region.

Brazil – children are used as slaves in forest clearance, charcoal burning and rubber tapping.

United Arab Emirates – children brought from south-east Asia and Africa are cruelly exploited as camel jockeys.

Sudan – children in the south are kidnapped and enslaved by government troops and used as farm labourers and for domestic work.

India, Nepal, Pakistan – hundreds of thousands of children as young as six or seven, are enslaved and work in the carpet industry.

 With a partner, make a list of all the human rights denied to these children.

 Write to your MSP with your concerns about these children.

 Can you find out more about child labour and/or slavery in these or other countries?

Map showing areas where child slavery exists

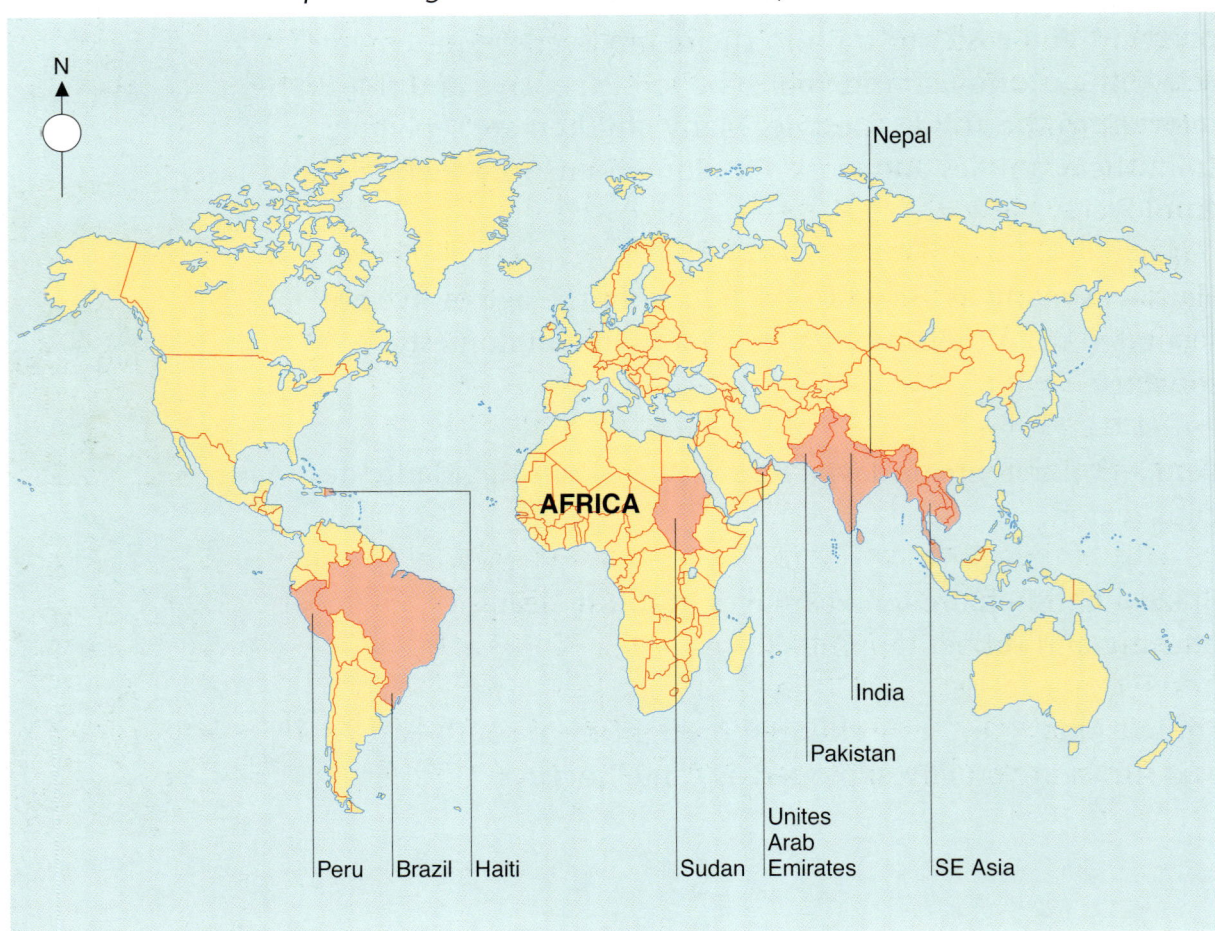

Working for the Rights of Others

Some people have spent their whole lives working for the rights of those who are oppressed – the poor, the old, the lonely. Very often these people believe so much in what they are doing that they are prepared to continue their work even when their own lives and personal safety are put at risk. They are concerned about the welfare of people and what will happen to them in the future. They speak and act on behalf of individuals or groups of people who for some reason are unable to speak for themselves. Here are some people who are working, or have worked, for the rights of others. Can you name them?

Find out about their lives. Why are they well known?

Martin Luther King was a black Baptist minister from the USA. When he became aware of the treatment of the black people in his country, he set out to lead them in a fight for their rights. In 1955, Mrs Rosa Parks refused to give up her seat on a bus to a white man, and was arrested. When Martin heard about this, he decided to take action. He became involved in a boycott of the buses. No black person would ride on the buses to work, town or school. The bus company was soon suffering from serious financial difficulties and, without a year, the US Supreme Court ruled that racial segregation on buses, seating black and white people in different parts of the bus, was against basic American laws. This started a campaign of non-violent resistance. He urged the black people to endure their suffering with quiet dignity. In this way he hoped to wear down the white authorities.

Martin Luther King suffered much himself, being imprisoned several times. He was stabbed in the chest. Finally he was assassinated by a white man, James Earl Ray. His greatness came from his total commitment to the principle of non-violent struggle. He succeeded in arousing a new awareness of the rights of black people and gave them hope of future freedom.

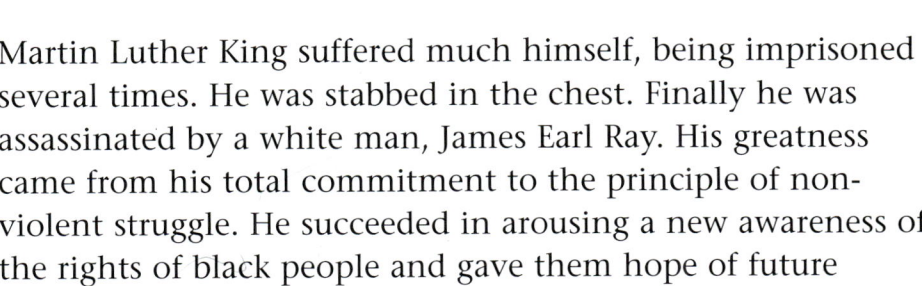

ACTIVITY

1 Work in groups. Act out the scene on the bus where Mrs Parks was arrested.

2 Come together and discuss the feelings of each character.

Mother Teresa

Mother Teresa was born in Yugoslavia in 1910. As a young woman she went to India to teach in a girls' school in Calcutta. The poorest people in India live in the slums of Calcutta, and she soon became aware of their terrible suffering and poverty and decided that she wanted to help. On Christmas Eve 1948, she started her work with the poor, and by the end of the day she had five orphans in her care. One week later she had 41 street children! She was joined by girls who wanted to help her, and she named them the Missionaries of Charity. Shocked when she found a woman barely alive on a rubbish tip, her body already decaying and infested by rats and insects, she set up a hospice for the dying. She wanted people to be able to die with dignity and to feel that they were wanted.

Sadly, Mother Teresa died in 1997. Mother Teresa's work has helped the poorest of the poor, whose poverty and wretched living conditions rob them of their dignity as human beings. The Missionaries of Charity spend their time working with them, continuing the work that Mother Teresa started.

ACTIVITY

1 Work in pairs and pretend it is 1990. One should pretend to be Mother Teresa and the other to be a reporter who wants to interview her about her life and work.

2 You could be an active citizen by organising a fund-raising event with your class, which would benefit a charity working for the rights of others, in this country or another.

CONSERVATION COUNTS

Election Fever

Beechwood Primary School Newsletter

Dear Parents,

Election fever has hit Beechwood Primary in a big way. We have just held our annual Pupil Council Election. The children have all worked extremely hard and I thought we would share all the interesting things they have done with you.

The Election Process:

Day 1   Application forms were accepted from any candidate in Primary 6 and 7. The children who wanted to be nominated worked at filling in their forms with assistance from their proposers and seconders.

Day 2   The Staff read the forms and chose the most suitable candidates from each house to take part in the election. This system gives the pupils the opportunity to belong to a particular group just like the political parties in a real election.

Day 3   What a wonderful hustings we had on day 3. The children rose to the occasion and promised the earth to their electorate in return for their vote!

BEECHWOOD PRIMARY

Pupil Council Election

Name	Proposer	Seconder

Reason for Standing

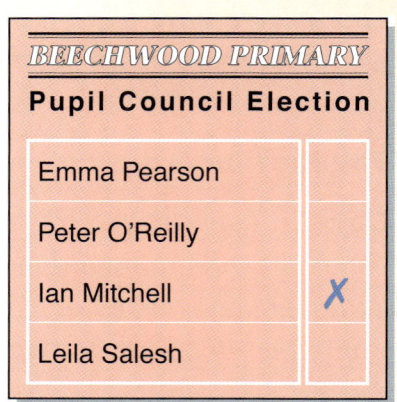

Campaigning was being carried out furiously. It made me smile when walking into school to see Alice, the lollipop lady with a 'Vote for Ian' sticker on her lollipop!

Day 4   Finally, the day of the election dawned and candidates were out in force rallying their voters. There was a ballot box for each house and the children cast their votes by marking an 'x', on their ballot paper opposite their chosen candidate.

Day 5   Excitement mounted as the ballot papers were counted and the election results announced.

Day 6   I am delighted to tell you that the 4 new captains who, along with our 4 eco-councillors, will make up the new Pupil Council in Beechwood Primary are: Ian Mitchell, Ayeesha Aziz, Ritchie Nimmo and Robyn Denholm.
I hope you enjoyed reading about our elections as much as we enjoyed holding them. Well done, children.

Mrs Liz Harris (Headteacher)

BEECHWOOD PRIMARY

Pupil Council Election

Emma Pearson	
Peter O'Reilly	
Ian Mitchell	X
Leila Salesh	

Do you have a house system, captains and/or a Pupil Council in your school? Discuss the similarities and differences between the election process in your school and the one in Beechwood.

The elected Pupil Council members represent the views of all the pupils in the school. Your local Councillor, MSP, MP and MEP represent the views of their electorate, the people who live in the place they represent.

Find out who is:
• Your local Councillor

CAREFUL DRIVERS ARE WELCOME IN BEECHWOOD

● Your Member of the Scottish Parliament

● Your Member of Parliament in Westminster

● Your Members of the European Parliament (Scotland)

Be an Active Citizen! Write to one of these people and tell them your views on a current issue. They need to know the views of the public in order to carry out their job properly. As a Citizen of the Future, your views are important.

Conservation counts!

The Pupil Council arrived for their monthly meeting. They took their places in the newly decorated school library. They sat down on the new chairs which were made from wood and covered in a wool fabric. The central heating was on and the room was lovely and warm. Around the room there was a TV and video, a CD player and several computers. When the children finished their meeting and went home from school they would play a video or computer game before having their dinner. Just another normal day in Beechwood or any other town...

 Make a list of all the things the Pupil Council take for granted in school and at home.

Which of these things do you own or expect to use?

Ask yourself what you would do without the everyday things that you take for granted.

We live in a consumer society and we believe our ability to survive depends on money to purchase the things we want.

 **Newsflash!** We have to look more towards the future and start looking after the resources provided for us by Planet Earth, rather than using them up without thinking of the consequences. This is Conservation.

Ask your teacher for the "Conservation Counts" game on Resource Sheet 14 to help you to understand more about conserving the Earth's resources.

The Pupil Council were aware of these issues and conservation was high on the agenda at their meeting.

ACTIVITY

YOUR MISSION IS . . .

Work in groups. Each group should choose an issue from the list to find out about:
- Pollution/waste
- Acid rain
- Global warming/Ozone layer
- Extinction of Rainforests or other habitats.

Use the Internet, books and other sources to research the facts. Discuss the facts in your own group.

Make a list of these on large sheets of paper and present your findings to the other groups in your class.

REMEMBER, THE EARTH'S FUTURE DEPENDS ON YOU!

It's important that you persuade Jack and others like him that

IT'S COOL TO BE A CONSERVATIONIST!

We may lose tomorrow unless more people take an active interest. We cannot leave the problem solving to the experts.

Become an **ACTIVE CITIZEN**, learn to use our natural resources without harming them.

Draw up an action plan

Here are some ideas to get you started:

1   Pollution and waste
FACT   The United States is top of the rubbish heap – each person there wastes 2 kg of materials every day.

- Take your old clothes to a charity shop.
- Share magazines with a friend.

2 Acid Rain

FACT   Wind, water and solar power are the renewable energy sources of the future.

- Use a calculator with a solar panel.
- Turn off lights when you are not using them.

3 Global Warming/Ozone Layer

FACT   In the 1980s it was discovered that holes were appearing in the Ozone layer.

- Don't buy fast food in cartons as they are usually made of polystyrene blown by CFCs.
- Buy pump action spray deodorants instead of aerosol sprays.

4 Destruction of the Rainforests and other Habitats

FACT   About half of all species of plants and animals live in the rainforest.

- Choosing new furniture for your bedroom? Choose a soft wood such as pine, oak, ash or beech.
- Don't pick wild flowers.
- Be careful that the souvenirs you bring back from your holidays are not made from scarce materials.

Before you begin, you should play "The Rainforest Game" — ask your teacher.

Guardians of the Globe

At the next meeting the Pupil Council drew up a 'Guardians of the Globe' Charter for their school. They wanted to be active citizens in protecting their environment.

Using the findings from your action plans, choose 6 areas which are important to your school and as a class, draw up your own Guardians Of the Globe Charter. You may decide to give it a different name. Whatever name you choose, in your group design a badge with a logo and create a catchy slogan to draw attention to your charter.

Taking Action

One of the issues on the Beechwood Charter was recycling because the Pupil Council had received complaints about litter in the playground and the amount of paper wasted within the school. Recycling would enhance the appearance of the school and save money at the same time. Discuss in groups the following information and see what else you can learn from the website: www.wasteonline.org.uk.

Recycling

We produce more rubbish today than ever before, on average each household in Britain produces about a tonne of waste every year. Much of this waste contains potentially useful materials such as paper and board, glass, metals and textiles which could be recycled, reducing the amount of rubbish, creating less pollution and saving energy.

Rubbish

The amount of rubbish we produce has been escalating over the last 40 years. There has been a gradual change in shopping habits and people's attitudes to throwing things away. The personal service provided by shop-keepers has been replaced by self-service in supermarkets where the goods are often highly packaged; often loose items are packed together and priced to speed up payment at the check-outs. Some goods are elaborately wrapped to make them look more attractive, put into plastic bags and then loaded into plastic carrier bags at the checkout. A Women's Environmental Network group bought a trolley-load of 102 basic items – the shopping for a family for two weeks. They found that there was a total of 543 pieces of packaging with some items wrapped in up to five layers!

On average a family of four throws away about two sacks of rubbish a week, most of which could be recycled. The figures below show the main constituents of household waste:

Paper and card 18%
Garden waste 21%
Kitchen waste 17%
Glass 7%
Metal and white goods 8%
Plastic 7%

The amounts are quite staggering. Each person in a year generates 10 times their own weight in household rubbish, throwing away an estimated 90 drink cans, 107 bottles and jars, two trees' worth of paper, 70 food cans and 45 kg of plastic.

Landfill

Almost 90% of domestic waste in the UK goes directly to landfill and dumping sites to be levelled and covered with earth. This costs about a million pounds every day.

This is an example of the governments' policy on domestic waste.

All governments make policy decisions, which affect the lives of the people in their country and sometimes worldwide. Here are other examples.

The curriculum (i.e. the subjects you learn in school) is decided upon by the Scottish Executive.

The amount of money taken from salaries for tax and national insurance is decided by the chancellor.

The decision to go to war is taken by the government of a country.

resource *sheet* Ask your teacher for the "Trash or Treasure Game" on Resource Sheet 15.

Recycling Enterprise

Primary 6 pupils at Beechwood school decided to turn their trash into treasure. They decided to make musical instruments from junk materials. They searched the Internet for instructions on how to make castanets, maracas, guiros, drums and other instruments.

By doing an Internet search, try to find these instructions for yourself. Once you have done that, in your group, try to make these instuments for yourself. Think carefully about the junk materials you will be able to use.

The Beechwood children wanted to raise money to donate to a Conservation Charity. They set up a company and called it 'Guardians of the Globe'. When planning their enterprise, they had to draw up a set of goals. To do this, they had to consider issues such as:

But the dilemma is...

PROFIT   versus   ETHICS

The Beechwood pupils wanted their enterprise to be successful, they wanted to make a profit but not at the expense of their Planet, and its people – remember, they were Guardians of the Globe!

The children had great fun making their instruments and putting on their concert. It was A GREAT SUCCESS!

In groups, consider the issues the Beechwood pupils highlighted. Relate each issue to Beechwood's enterprise. Report back on how successful they were in meeting their goals. Was 'Guardians of the Globe' an ethical enterprise?

DEVELOPING COUNTRIES

7

Introduction

Beechwood Press

ocal couple Joe and Marion Briggs have just returned from a visit to Peru. While there, they were deeply affected by the conditions under which many people are living. In a village north of Lima, 3000 families live on desert slopes, in houses made of straw matting. Some have bricks and wood but no cement. Mrs Briggs was invited into a typical home and told our reporter how humbled she felt when she realised how little these families had. There were no tables, chairs or the many electrical items which we take for granted. Instead she saw a bed, a stove for cooking, a few utensils and an oil lamp. The floor of the house was exactly the same as the desert outside. Electric meters stood in the street, and toilets were no more than a hole in the ground. No one can ever remember it raining in the village, and water is brought in by lorry. Each house has a large drum which can be filled for a few sols (the local money). They saw a group of young women sharing a tub of water to wash their clothes. Mr Brigs, a keen gardener, said it would take a miracle for anything to grow there as there was no soil, only sand. This means no food can be grown and malnourishment is a serious problem. As a result of this, children look younger than they are, while adults look much older.

As they passed the school it was time for the seniors to finish their day, but time for the infants and juniors to start. Shortage of space means not everyone can go to school at the same time.

Mr and Mrs Briggs are hoping to do some fund-raising in order to help the people in this Peruvian village.

What help do you think the village people need?

Can you think of any ways in which money could be raised to help them?

Make two lists, one naming the things in the house which Mrs Briggs visited, and another for your own house.

Discuss the difficulties the people in the Peruvian village face daily.

How often do you use water every day?

Think of ways in which you could cut down on water usage if you had to.

Aid to Others

Malnutrition is a problem in many parts of the world. Other nations can help by supplying food; this is known as short-term aid. Mr and Mrs Briggs saw women in the Peruvian village preparing meals for the hungry. The food for this is usually donated by charities. Rice came from America and flour from Scandinavia. Some children got a breakfast of porridge at school, which was made from dried milk donations from Denmark.

ACTIVITY

Can you think of occasions when food has been asked for in a crisis situation? You may want to look in newspapers for evidence of aid being given at present.

Short-term aid could also be clothes, medicine, toiletries or anything else required to help solve a problem immediately. Short-term aid is good, but is sometimes not the answer to the problem – it will not stop the problem from happening again.

Consider each of the following forms of long-term aid:

1. Helping small farmers own the land they work on.

2. Providing machinery.

3. Providing expertise.

4. Teaching new skills and encouraging traditional skills.

5. Helping to cancel the national debt (the amount one country owes to others).

6. Providing seeds and tools.

7. Helping farmers to get their crops to market and get a fair price.

8. Sinking wells and supplying pumps, pipes and taps.

9. Providing a desalination plant (to provide fresh water).

10. Helping trade – providing a market for goods.

11. Working for democracy (government by the people) in order that people can change bad governments.

12. Encouraging governments to spend money on developments, not weapons.

Decide which would help the people in the Peruvian village.

Why Are So Many People Hungry?

1. In my country there is a lot of war. It has been like this for many years. Our crops don't get a chance to grow and we have to keep moving.

2. In my country we haven't had rain for many years, and the rivers and lakes have all dried up. We plant crops but they die.

3. In my country all our trees have been chopped down. Now when it rains there are no roots to hold the soil together. The water runs down the hillsides and drowns the crops below.

4. My country owes a lot of money to other countries, so the government forces us to grow crops which other countries want to buy, such as coffee, tea, tobacco and cocoa.

5. We have plenty to eat in our country, but rather than sell certain foods cheaply, we produce less to keep the prices high. Sometimes 'food mountains' develop when we have extra.

Match each of the following words with the situations shown opposite.

| Uneven shares | Flood | Cash crops | Drought | Conflict |

In your group, choose a word from the box and use it to do an Internet search to help you find out about countries where the conditions mentioned exist.

Cash Crops – A Case Study

Lucia is nearly 5 years old. She lives with her family on a sugar plantation on one of the islands in the Philippines. Her father, Ramone, worked for Mr Nolan, the owner of the sugar plantation. Mr Nolan made sure his workers depended on him. They had to buy all their food from his shop. The food had to be imported from other places because all the land was used for growing sugar. Sugar was a cash crop for the Philippines. It was because the demand for sugar from rich countries like the USA was high, that countries like the Philippines gave up growing food for their own people and started growing crops such as sugar to export.

Mr Nolan was a rich landowner whose employees were poorly paid. The workers lived on Mr Nolan's land but the houses had no electricity or water. Lucia's older sister, Helena, spent at least 2 hours a day collecting water from a tap used by 50 other families. These families were always in debt because there was no work on the plantation and therefore no wages from May to September. Life was hard for Lucia and her family.

Two years ago, Ramone lost his job because the price Mr Nolan could get for his sugar fell so low it was no longer worth harvesting it.

Sugar cane is one of the oldest cash crops. However, during the First World War, when countries couldn't get their usual imports of sugar, they started to produce their own sugar from home grown sugar beet and sweeteners from home grown maize. Gradually, sugar from islands like Lucia's wasn't needed any more. Because the islanders, and others for whom sugar was a cash crop, couldn't grow their own food and had no other means of earning money, they suffered great hardship. Poor Lucia became so undernourished, her parents thought she would die.

Lucia's story is typical of many families who relied on cash crops for their existence.

resource sheet

Other cash crops are bananas, tea and coffee. To show you an example of what can happen when people have to grow cash crops, ask your teacher for "The Banana Game" on Resource Sheet 16.

Helping Themselves

Although conditions in the village were poor, Mr and Mrs Briggs saw evidence that the people were trying to overcome the difficulties facing them. The major problems in trying to grow food are lack of soil and no rainfall, but Mr and Mrs Briggs did see plants, vegetables, flowers, herbs and shrubs all growing within the village. The idea was taken from a successful hydroponics programme in Israel where a lot of the land is also desert. 'Hydroponics' means growing plants without soil. Plants are placed in special containers which allow them to dip their roots into a solution of water and fertiliser. The water is recycled. This gives fresh food, a source of income, and employs some local workers. They hope to expand this programme by purchasing a lorry which will let them take their produce to the market in Lima.

Many other poor countries are trying to overcome similar difficulties. These countries are often known as 'developing countries' or 'the third world'. You can see these on the map.

N

Third world countries

Not all plants like the same soils, temperatures or amounts of water, so different plants grow in different parts of the world depending on the conditions they need. The difficulties are growing the correct type of food, growing enough food, and getting it to the people who need it.

Look at this list of foods which are all grown in developing countries:

rice	yams	plantain
sugar cane	maize	bulgar wheat
coconuts	quinoa	wheat noodles

Find out which developing country they are grown in.

Choose one of these countries and plan an investigation, asking questions like:

What are the problems the people face?

Why are they poor? What is their lifestyle like?

In what way is it different from your own? Do they have enough to eat? What factors affect their ability to grow food?

Does this country receive any form(s) of aid?

Aid Agencies

Within the third world many of the people are trying to improve their way of life. Agencies based in richer countries help them get a fair price for their goods. Many of the problems in the third world exist because the people are exploited by employers who pay very little, governments who say what they can plant, and companies which pay very little for their goods but sell them at huge profits.

Life has improved for Ramena. She lives in a village in India and is a member of a co-operative which helped her by giving her a loan of money to buy materials when she started her basket-weaving business. This co-operative provides training and advice on designs, then sells the work all over the world at a fair price. Many supermarkets are now selling fairly-traided goods which were grown or made in third world countries and then brought to the UK for sale.

Can you think of any organisations which sell goods from third world countries?

Conduct a survey to find out which charities are supported by people you know. Plan your question and answer sheet before you start. Are you going to provide a list of charities so that people can identify which ones they support by a tick? Or are you going to ask them to write down the names of the charities? Which will be easiest for people to use and for you to collate?

How will you report your findings?

Which charities does your school support, and how do you support them?

Fair Trade

Fair trade means:

- paying fair prices for produce from the third world;
- giving credit where needed;
- working together to build a better future.

Traidcraft is an organisation working for a fairer way of trading with groups in Africa, Asia and Latin America. It is a business based on co-operation not exploitation, with a commitment to respect the skills, traditions and hard work of third world producers.

Here are some items from a Traidcraft catalogue. The catalogue also contains interesting information. Use the information on these pages to do the tasks on Resource Sheet 17.

Ask your teacher for Resource Sheet 17.

Cafédirect Instant 5065 Premium Coffee

5065 is the 'height of coffee taste'. Blended from high quality beans from Latin America and Africa. 5065 is a premium instant coffee. A smooth high quality taste with a great aroma that can be made in an instant, allowing you to enjoy it any time.

Traidcraft coffees are sourced from small farmers' co-operatives and come from farms in Peru, Mexico, Costa Rica, Nicaragua, Dominican Republic, Haiti, Cameroon, Tanzania and Uganda.

Divine Chocolate

Divine milk chocolate made with cocoa from Ghana. Contains real cocoa butter and vanilla.

937 village societies make up the 'Kuapa Kokoo' union of farmers in Ghana who produce the cocoa for this chocolate. They currently sell about 650 tonnes of cocoa to the fair trade market each year. Comfort Kwaasibea, a member of Kuapa Kokoo says

Comfort Kwaasibea

'*Through fair trade and Kuapa we now have good drinking water, toilet facilities and schools. We meet every two weeks to share our problems and we are all involved in deciding how our fair trade premium is spent.*'

Serving Dish

A stunningly stylish, glazed, stoneware oven-proof serving dish made in Indonesia using a traditional, hand-thrown method. Suitable for oven use. Dishwasher and microwave safe. 19.5cm top diameter, 8cm deep.

'Arum Dalu' is the name of the company who produced this serving dish. It was set up by Tommy Fredrickson with Sarie, an Indonesian handcraft expert. They work closely with producers to help develop new products like this one. Arum Dalu is currently working with 25–30 groups over a wide range of handicrafts.

Camel Burmese Shawl

This exceptional fringed shawl is the perfect present to make someone feel special. Close up you can truly appreciate the outstanding weaving skills and its intricate diamond pattern. By buying fair trade items like this, you can help to sustain traditions, which are important to local artisans' culture and livelihood. 100% rayon. 194 × 42cm.

Thaicraft is a non-profit organisation which was set up in 1992 to work with artisan groups, help them gain self-reliance and to preserve Thailand's indigenous crafts.

La-ong sells silver beads through Thaicraft to support her three children and send her two sons, Ting and Tee, to school. She says

'Thank you for buying traditional crafts from us. We have a job because of you.'

La-ong
Jasda Trivittayanuruk

Festival Elephant

This colourful hand-painted rubberwood puzzle, when completed, looks great leading a procession of toys along a child's bedroom floor. From an organisation in Sri Lanka training uneducated young people into employment. Unsuitable for children under 3 years, contains small parts. 21 × 14.5cm.

Since 1977, Gospel House Handicrafts have given employment and training to the poor areas of Colombo and other areas of Sri Lanka. Their toy factory at Madampe provides work for 35 young people and the group employs 115 producers in total.

Butterfly Beaded Hairclips (2)

Two, gorgeously girly metal hairclips brightly beaded into butterfly shapes. Handmade in India. Each clip 7cm long.

These clips are one of many products made by Tara Projects in India. This is a non-profit organisation, based in Delhi, which represents 25 community-based groups of craft workers from all over North India. They are Traidcraft's biggest supplier of crafts and their aim is to help craft workers to become self-sufficient by giving them the skills to make and sell their own products. Master craftsman Mohd Usman explains that life for his family has changed since they have begun to sell their goods through fair trade:

Mohd Usman

'We were not prosperous and did not get money on time. We were in debt. It was a very hard time. When we came into contact with Tara Projects our lives changed. We have already paid off our debt and have saved some money for our daughters' marriages.'

ACTIVITY

Work in groups. Use the Internet to find:
- Indian sitar music
- An Indian recipe
- Indian costumes
- Indian crafts.

Once you have gathered this information your class could display some of it and celebrate Indian culture by having your own festival.

THE COMMUNITY CENTRE

Introduction: Sources of Funding

The local council decided that it would be an advantage to Beechwood if there was a Community Centre where meetings could be held and which clubs could use. Until now, groups had been using schools, but it was becoming difficult to find times to suit everyone. People wanting to use sports facilities had to travel to Silverton, some distance away, which was difficult for those who didn't have cars.

There were a few possible sites in the area, but the first thing the council had to consider was how they would fund the building and running of a Centre.

 **ACTIVITY**

In groups:

1. Consider ways in which the money for the Centre could be obtained.

2. What uses could a Community Centre have?

83

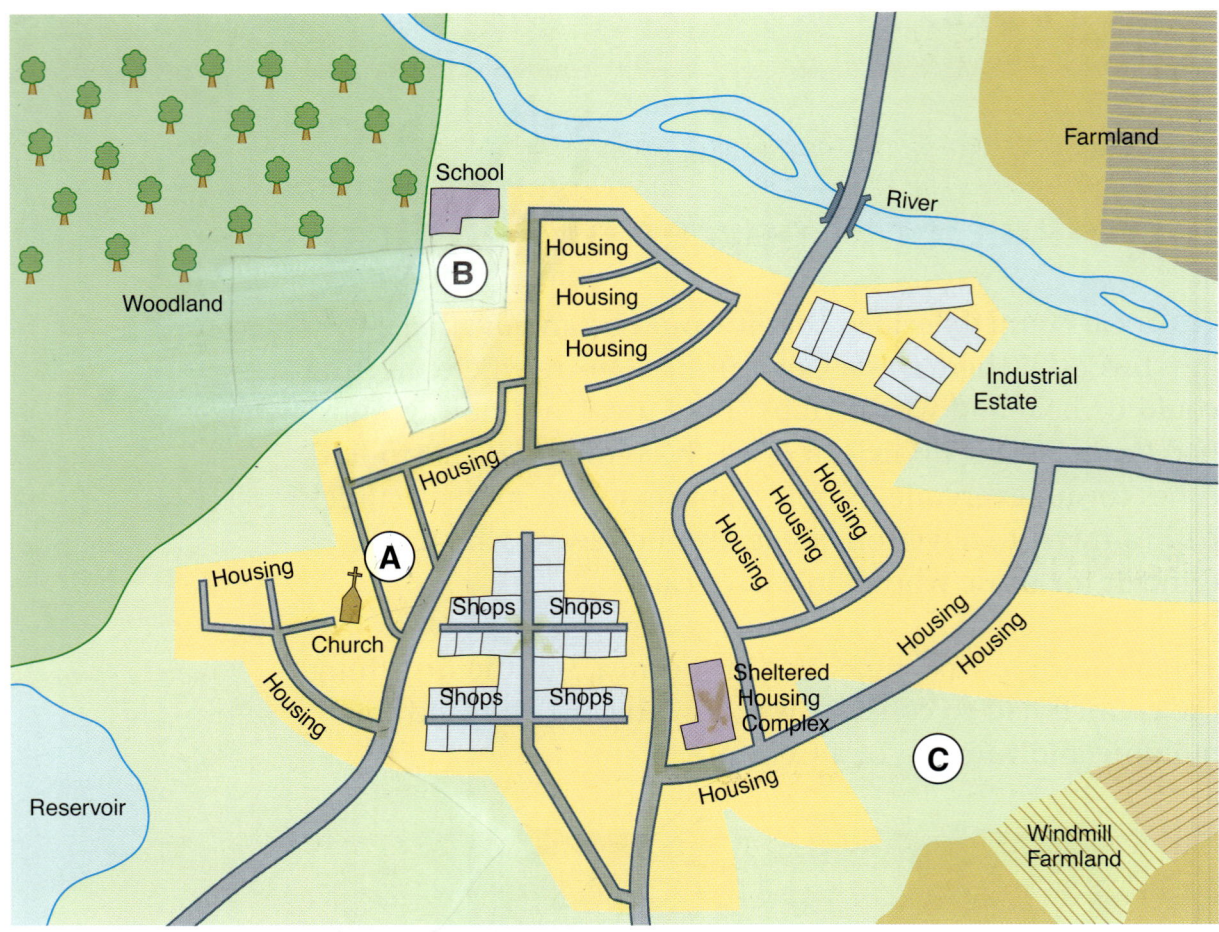

Choosing a Site for the Centre

Having acquired funding for the Centre, the council had to consider possible sites. While doing this they had to consider:

a) the size of the site – will there be enough ground for a car/coach park? Do they want outdoor facilities?

b) what will be the best location for the community? How will the building of the Centre affect people?

c) how easy will it be for people to reach the Centre by car, bus, train etc.?

d) the cost involved if they have to put in gas connections, new roads etc.

e) if the ground would be suitable for building? Test bores will have to be done to make sure the ground is safe.

ACTIVITY

1. Look at the map of Beechwood and consider the advantages and disadvantages of the possible sites. Make a checklist of reasons for and against each site.

2. Once you have finished, ask your teacher for Resource Sheet 18 and compare the information with your list.

3. As a class, make a decision on which site you would select.

Making Plans

When people heard that a Community Centre was going to be built in the town, there were mixed feelings.

Farmer McLean: 'I don't want the Centre near my land.'

Schoolgirls: 'I hope it's near the school'; 'Perhaps it will have a swimming pool.'

Wildlife Ranger: 'There are badgers in the woodland that must be protected.'

Young mum: 'I hope it's in the town centre where I can make full use of the facilities.'

Proprietor of coach firm: 'If the site is on the outskirts of the town I can run buses to it.'

Minister: 'There is a conservation order on the abbey.'

Group of young parents: 'We don't want an access road through our housing estate.'

Canoeist: 'I hope they choose the site near the river.'

Councillor: 'We will take everyone's views into consideration.'

After a lot of consideration the council decided on site C, as site A wasn't large enough and the ground on site B was found to be unsuitable when the results of the test bore were studied.

The council were also worried about the effect on the only area of woodland in the surrounding district.

Make a list of amenities in your local area. Remember to include things like bus stops, post boxes etc.

Where are they situated?

Who in your class has most amenities near his/her home?

Where in your local area would be a good site for a new Community Centre? Make sure your site is eco-friendly.

The council want as many people as possible to use the Centre. Therefore, they have to think about what facilities different age groups will want.

To do this they may be involved in research to discover what people want and what facilities are already available.

- hall
- gym
- swimming pool
- library
- badminton courts
- sauna
- kitchen etc.

ACTIVITY

1 Design a questionnaire which will help you to find out what people want in a Community Centre. Try out your questionnaire on people you know. Remember to ask people from different age-groups.

2 Compare your findings with others.

resource *sheet*

Ask your teacher for Resource Sheet 19, showing a detailed questionnaire.

It may not be possible to fulfil all the expectations, and the council may have to prioritise and make decisions.

3 As a class, decide what you would have in your Centre if you only have enough money for five major things.

4 Design a Centre with the things your class choose in it.

Remember to label and explain your plans.

Fire Safety

All new buildings have to comply with the registered standards which are set out by the Scottish Office in order that the building will be safe. The plans are given to the Fire Safety Officer, who will check that they meet the necessary requirements.

ACTIVITY

1 Describe your school fire drill. What rules do you follow? Take a look around your school and note what safety equipment or procedures you can find.

2 Use or draw a plan of the ground floor of your school and put in corridors, classrooms, hall, gym, dining room etc.

3 Use a highlighter and write 'Fire exit' at the correct points.

4 Using the same colour, mark in the exit route you would take if there was a fire in your school.

5 How many exit routes did you find?

6 How many different types of fire extinguisher does your school have? Where are they positioned? Why are they different? Find out about the different types and their uses. The Internet would be a good place to start your search.

7 Now look carefully at your Community Centre plans. Is your Centre going to be a safe place for employees and the public? Think about what safety features will be required and highlight these on your plan.

8 Write out a fire procedure for the Centre.

Informing the Public

At this point the group decided to hold a public meeting where they could exhibit the plans for the Centre and answer any questions. Public meetings like this are often held to inform people about proposed projects and try to convince them that they are good ideas. Beechwood Council wanted to let as many people as possible know all about the Centre and how it would benefit the community. The more people who supported the idea, the fewer objections it would mean when they applied for planning permission.

ACTIVITY

In groups, prepare a presentation for the site Beechwood Council has chosen.

- You want to encourage people to accept your plans for the Centre.
- Everyone in the group must have a job to do.
- It is important to stick to your agreed task.
- Try to think of different and unusual ways of presenting your information.

- Make sure your visual information is clearly and neatly labelled, is eye-catching, and appeals to your audience.
- Those whom you have chosen to give the oral presentation must be well prepared, speak clearly and remain within an agreed time limit.
- Remember, you are trying to convince the public that this is a great idea!

Getting the Go-ahead

Once the design has been decided, the committee has to submit:

1 A planning application.

The planning application deals with traffic control, how much parking space is planned, the appearance of the building and its location.

When looking at location, the effect of the Centre on housing, other developments and the environment must be considered.

People in the area around the planned site must be notified. This is done by writing letters to them.

Notice of application is also placed in the local paper and a notice is erected on the site.

Any objections have to be sent to the planning department.

2 An application for a building warrant from the building control department.

When the application for a building warrant is submitted, the drawings and maps are checked to make sure the plans meet all the necessary standards.

Ask your teacher for Resource Sheet 20, which is a planning application form. Fill in the form for your site.

To Be or Not to Be

When the site for the Centre was announced, some people were very relieved that it wasn't going to be near them; some people were disappointed that it wasn't going to be near them; some people thought it was the perfect choice; and others weren't happy at all!

Proprietor of coach firm: 'This will be good for business.'

Minister: 'The abbey will be safe.'

Wildlife Ranger: 'I'm glad the woods and animals will not be affected.'

Canoeist: 'I'm disappointed that there are not going to be water sports facilities.'

Schoolgirls: 'We would have preferred site B because it was so handy for the school, but we'll still go.'

Young mum: 'If the centre had been nearer the shops I could have used it when I was shopping and saved myself an extra journey. I never have enough time as it is.'

The people in the sheltered housing complex, the houses nearest site C, and Mr McLean of Windmill Farm are angry that this site has been chosen.

They will have to write to the planning department stating their objections.

However, they could also get together to discuss a campaign which will let people know why they are unhappy and to stop the building from going ahead.

ACTIVITY

Imagine you are in this group.

1 Consider other ways in which you can let people know your feelings and whom you can contact.

2 Plan a campaign to publicise your views.

3 Look at the objections to location C and write a letter to the planning department or to one of the people who may be able to help your campaign.

4 Plan a public meeting where members of the community will have the opportunity to express their different views.

Each member of your group/class can take part in this role-play activity as either an organiser, a speaker or a member of the audience.

You will need people for and against the site, and a chairperson. Here are some other roles you may want to include: council representatives, someone from the planning department, a police representative, a local MP, someone from the Ministry of Agriculture, a local newspaper reporter, and any of the other people you think could help your campaign.

ACTIVITY

Before the protest meeting:

1. Look back at the map and all the information you have on the proposed site, and consider again how the position of the Centre will affect you.

2. Make careful notes of what you are going to say at the meeting.

3. Make sure all necessary arrangements have been made, for example, posters, handouts, displays.

The planning department will meet and consider whether to:

a)   approve the plan
b)   alter it if there are objections
c)   reject the plan.

On the Site

When permission has been granted, the architect supervises the work, but other people are involved.

The quantity surveyor measures the amount of work, for example, how many bricks are needed, how much plaster is required, how much time will be involved. He then draws up the contract, which he puts out to tender. This means that firms who are interested put in offers of how much money they would charge to do the job. Often the cheapest gets the contract, although quality checks are made to make sure the firm is reliable. The architect will supervise the work and check it at different stages. The building control department will also check the building at different stages, for example, the foundations will be checked before the builders can continue, and a certificate will be issued when the building is complete to show it meets all standards.

There are three main kinds of people involved in the Community Centre:

1. **Primary workers.** These are the people who collect the raw materials for the Centre, e.g. sand from a quarry.
2. **Secondary workers.** These are the people who use the raw materials to build the Centre, car parks etc, e.g. bricklayers.
3. **Tertiary workers.** These are the people who will make sure the Centre runs smoothly, e.g. the caretaker.

ACTIVITY

1 Make a list of all the people you think will be involved in building the Centre.

2 Choose three and describe what they do. You may have to research in various ways.

3 Discuss fairness in employment (wages, hours, discrimination).

Hiring Staff

When the Centre is completed, people have to be employed. The number of staff will depend on the facilities provided and on the money available for wages.

Who will be needed?

Who is employed in Centres that you go to?

What type of people would you be looking for?

How many people would you have to employ for your Centre?

The jobs were advertised in the Job Centre and in the local paper, and soon people were sending for application forms and returning them for the posts they were interested in. Graeme

Anderson applied for the post of Reception Manager and enclosed a curriculum vitae or CV as it is often known. In a CV, applicants give as much relevant information as they can about themselves, their education and qualifications which they have. Here is Graeme's CV:

Curriculum Vitae

My name is Graeme Anderson. I am 23 years old.

Qualifications: Standard grade in English, Maths, Modern Studies and PE.

Scotvec modules in computing and communications.

Present position: Sales assistant in large bookshop.

Previous experience: Saturday job in local superstore.

Skills: Competent on computer. Trained on filing systems in present job.

Qualities: I have shown in my present position that I can be trusted to handle large amounts of money. My approach to the public is businesslike but friendly. I have a clear speaking voice. I hold a clean driving licence.

Hobbies: I enjoy most sports and participate regularly in badminton and football. I assist with a scout troop and I am a volunteer DJ with the local hospital radio.

Any other relevant information: As I live locally and know many of the residents of Beechwood, I feel I would be an asset to the Centre.

ACTIVITY

1   Working in pairs, list the qualities Graeme has which would be useful in the job he has applied for.

2   Is there anything in Graeme's CV which would make him unsuitable for the post? You may not find anything, as people try to be positive in what they are saying in a CV in order to get an interview.

3   CVs give certain information about a person. Look at the headings on Graeme's CV. Start a CV for yourself, filling in the information which applies to you, or imagine that you are applying for one of the posts in your Centre.

Rules and Logos

Once the staff are in place, they have to look at how the Centre will be run.

Rules are always necessary for the efficient, fair and safe operation of any group. What groups are you involved in or do you belong to, which require rules?

Beechwood Centre will be no different. It will need rules too.

In groups, make a list of any rules you can think of which will help run the Centre:

a)   smoothly

b)   fairly

c)   safely.

As a class, compare your lists and decide on which ones you would have in your Centre.

Many organisations use logos such as these:

New Lanark Conservation Trust
Strathclyde Country Park
Yellow Pages
Scottish Tourist Board
Deep Sea World

The design reflects the purpose or message of the organisation.
Why has each organisation chosen its particular logo?

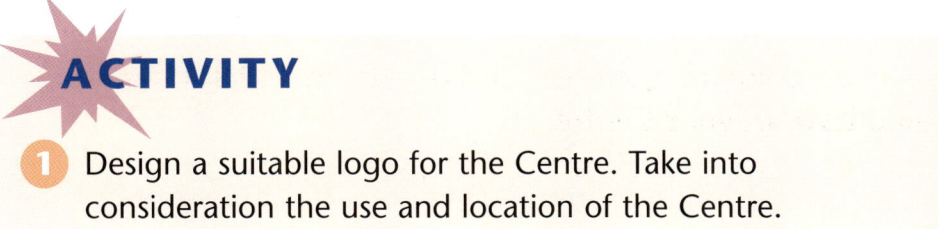

ACTIVITY

1 Design a suitable logo for the Centre. Take into
consideration the use and location of the Centre.

Membership

Everyone can use the Centre but, as a bonus to the people of Beechwood, the management are considering having a membership scheme where local people will be given priority. Many Centres allow local people to make advance bookings.

Do you think this is fair?

What other benefits could a membership scheme offer?

Would everyone pay the same entry fees or would you have concessions?

Who would be concessionary members?

ACTIVITY

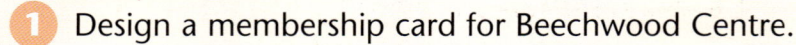

1. Design a membership card for Beechwood Centre.

2. How could you stop people from lending their membership cards to others who haven't got their own?

3. Will people pay for membership?

As a lot of groups will be using the Centre, the management will have to make a timetable to avoid problems. To do this, they have to consider the uses of the various sections of the Centre and the time allowed for each session, which may vary with the different activities or 'lets' (bookings). They have decided that the opening times for the Centre will be:

Monday–Friday: 9 am – 9 pm.   Saturday–Sunday:
                                 10 am – 4 pm.

The management have already decided that on Saturday evenings the hall should be available for functions such as parties or wedding receptions. Therefore, no other groups can book the hall at these times.

ACTIVITY

Working with a partner, help the management to draw up a timetable for the Centre's main hall. The following applications for lets have already been received:

Senior Citizens want to book it Monday to Friday from 12 noon until 2 pm for a luncheon club.

Girl Guides: Tuesday and Thursday 2 hours each evening.

Brownies: Wednesday 2 hours.

Football: Saturday pm 1 hour and Sunday am 1 hour.

Keep Fit: 1 morning session of 1 hour.
1 evening session of 1 hour.

Badminton Club: Saturday am 1 hour and 1 evening 2-hour session.

Tea Dancing: 1 afternoon, 2 hours.

Parents and Toddlers: 2 morning sessions of 2 hours each.

Line Dancing: 1 morning session of 2 hours.
1 evening session of 2 hours.

After School Club: Monday–Friday 2 hours each day.

Could you add in any activities, which you thought of having in the main hall of your Centre?

Opening Day

At last the Centre is complete, staff have been employed, timetables are completed, and the management is organising a grand opening day.

How would you go about organising it?

Consider:

1 Who would you invite?

2 Who would officially open it? (Who could you afford? Will you choose a famous person or a local person?)

3 What format would the celebration take?

4 Would catering be required? Who would do it? Would the food be the same for everyone? (Would special guests have something different?) Would you have a sit-down meal or a buffet?

5 Would there be entertainment? What things might influence your decisions?

ACTIVITY

1 The following three menus were received from companies interested in catering for the Opening Reception. Look carefully at each one and decide which you would use.

Ask your teacher for your budget for the catering and for the prices which the companies have quoted. Discuss your options and the advantages and disadvantages of each.

MENU 1

Courgette soup
Fanned melon with seasonal fruit
Scottish oatcakes with country pâté

****

Roast sirloin of Scottish beef
Chicken Kiev
York ham salad
Vegetable salad

****

Selection of seasonal vegetables

****

Black Forest gateau
Apple pie with cream

****

Coffee and after-dinner mints

MENU 2

Sausage rolls
Sandwiches – gammon, egg, chicken
Chicken drumsticks
Cheese and egg flan
Tuna pasties
Selection of cold meats
Various salads

****

Selection of gateaux

MENU 3

Minced pork en croute
Sandwich platter – honey roast ham bridge rolls:
egg mayonnaise croissants: chicken tikka and
brown bread parcels
Seafood vol-au-vents
Platter of freshly carved roasts
Pasta, prawn and apple salad, Waldorf salad,
curried rice salad ring

·······

Chocolate and vanilla roulade
Raspberry torte
Lemon and kiwi cheesecake

ACTIVITY

1 In a small group, plan the opening day for the Centre.
Remember that the organisers would have to work within
a budget, and therefore any decisions must be made with
this in mind. Display your plans in an attractive way for the
others in your class to see.